'Twas the Night Before Christmas

ISBN 978-1-0980-2355-3 (paperback)
ISBN 978-1-0980-2356-0 (digital)

Christian Faith Publishing, Inc.
832 Park Avenue
Meadville, PA 16335
www.christianfaithpublishing.com

Printed in the United States of America

'Twas the Night Before Christmas

A Story of Love

Illustrations by Gabe Sappenfield

JONI LOYLAND PRATER

’Twas the night before Christmas in old Bethlehem,
Joseph knocked on the door,
“Kind sir, may we please come in?

My wife is with child, we're hungry and cold!"
But the innkeeper said, "Every room has been sold."

I'm afraid to go on, I think the baby's time is near.

Joseph turned in despair, Mary's eyes shed a tear.

"I'm afraid to go on.

I think the baby's time is near."

He knelt down beside her and bowed his head low.

"Dear Father, please help us, we've no where to go."

The door slowly opened, the innkeeper appeared.
"There's room in the stable,
But it's cold there, I fear.
Please take a blanket and a small candlelight.
At least you can rest on this cold winter's night."

Mary smiled so softly and held Joseph's hand.
They walked in the moonlight,
Trudging slowly through sand.
"Don't worry, my darling, God's with us," he said.
And he lay down the blanket on the hay for a bed.

When Mary's time came for her child to be born,

Joseph covered her gently with the coat he had worn.

He cradled her head and stroked her long hair

And God eased the pain for the child she would bear.

While the cows gently mooed, sheep baaed, and horses neighed
A Savior was born, and in a manger he lay.
While his mother sang softly and rocked him to sleep,
The angels watched over the promise God would keep.

Nearby, there were shepherds
Keeping watch o'er flocks by night,
And the angel appeared in a glorious light!
"Go see what has happened in quaint Bethlehem.
A Savior is born—you must go worship him!"

A bright shining star marked the place where he lay,
And the three wise men searched
'Til they came to the babe.
They worshipped the King as the prophets had told
And gave him their gifts of myrrh, frankincense, and gold.

’Tis the night before Christmas, and how thankful we are
For sweet baby Jesus and the bright shining star
That showed them the stable
Where the Savior did lay
And led them to worship as we do here today.

Come, let us adore him.
Hark, the herald angels sing!
For this babe in a manger
Is our Savior, our King!

May we always remember how
God's love shone that night
Between Mary and Joseph and
angels of light.

May we come like the shepherds,
Bow down like the wise men,
For the true gift of Christmas is Jesus.
Amen.

About the Author

Passioned by an incessant entrepreneurial spirit that focuses on creativity, Joni Prater has been a pastry chef, owner of a European bakery, caterer, florist, digital embroiderer, and weaver. Two constants in her life are her love for reading and a love for kids. As a proud mother to four adult children, adoring grandmother to two little ones, and a former Sunday School teacher, she has 40 years of joyful experience relating to children and helping them grow into their best selves. She lives in Austin, Texas with her two rescue pups, Gracie and Lucy.

Joni wrote this poem 20 years ago when she wanted her preschool Sunday School class to experience the story of Christmas, so she set out to bring the pages to life and help them better understand and cherish this beautiful story. Several of the students and fellow teachers have told her they display the original poem in their homes every Christmas. She hopes it will become a tradition in your home too.

CPSIA information can be obtained
at www.ICGtesting.com
Printed in the USA
LVHW051608141020
668653LV00013B/166